GOD,
you've
got
to be
kidding

GOD,
you've got to be kidding

Cal LeMon

Creation House
Carol Stream, Illinois

Biblical quotations, unless otherwise indicated, are from the *New American Standard Bible,* © 1971 by the Lockman Foundation, and are used with permission.

International Standard Book Number 0-88419-049-8
Library of Congress Catalog Number 73-81983

To Rev. and Mrs. Robert E. LeMon, Sr.,
who lived the law in our house
along with enforcing it.

Contents

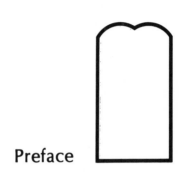

Preface

Since 1971 I have had the opportunity to minister to a collegiate congregation. There they've been—every Tuesday morning, twelve hundred of them. What has frightened me most is their refusal to just sit there, sleep, or read textbooks. They seem like cassettes, recording my words to challenge my logic and creativity.

Oh, how these kids make me work! Nights of digging in the Scriptures to feed this voracious young crowd...I love it. They provide the discipline for me to search and define biblical ideas for both sides of the pulpit.

It was in this context that I preached a series of sermons on the Ten Commandments. I wanted to discover the contemporary implications of the Law and find application for the Christian collegian. In these next pages you will hear a lot about the people and campus I know best, but the loudest voice, hopefully, will be that of the Holy Spirit as He directs your ethical decisions. Thanks for taking time to share this experience with me.

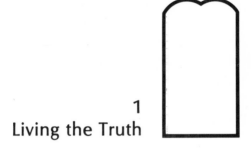

1
Living the Truth

Have you ever been ashamed to wear your college sweatshirt? When I was a student* at Evangel College in Springfield, Missouri, I had this baggy maroon rag with the college seal on the front of it. You couldn't see the name unless you looked closely, but you couldn't miss the big word in the middle: *TRUTH*. Do you believe it?! *Truth*.

During summer vacations I'd go home

---

*LeMon is now chaplain at his alma mater, where he first developed the content of this book for use with students.

to Atlantic City, New Jersey, and wear my sweatshirt on the world-famous Boardwalk. Thousands of other students would be there with sweatshirts that read, "Harvard Football," "Penn State," and "Dartmouth Wrestling." Before long I decided maybe my truth-shirt would look better inside out.

But at college I knew all about truth. Truth was so popular it was sold in the campus bookstore: I took class notes with truth-pens on truth-notebooks; my books were covered with truth-bookcovers accented by gold truth-bookmarks. A student could even purchase a questionable-looking truth-mug. Truth was lastingly imprinted on our belongings, but unfortunately, not on our minds and hearts.

Many men through the years have tried to define truth. Ben Johnson said it is "man's proper good;" Emerson saw truth as the "summit of being," while Huxley observed truth as the "heart of morality." Yet, the question of what the ultimate truth is continues to haunt humanity.

The unrewarded pursuit of truth has left us in an age wallowing in despair. Our popular music blaringly shouts it these days. When the truth of life cannot be found, death by despair is inevitable.

But listen to the Christians: "We know the ultimate truth!" Where do they get the brass to make such a blatant assertion? Christians say Truth, with a capital *T,* is Jesus Christ. He's the Truth because in Him is found the answer to the riddle of life. They shout John 14:6 back to Jean Paul Sartre and his coterie of despair: "I am the way, and the truth, and the life." They live in the pride and assurance of that claim by their Lord.

Yet Paul said it was not enough for us to know the truth; it must be acted out on the stages of our lives. "But we have renounced the things hidden because of shame, not walking in craftiness or adulterating the word of God, but by the manifestation of truth commending ourselves to every man's conscience in the sight of God," he wrote in 2 Corinthians 4:2. When Paul says, "manifestation of truth," he uses the Greek verb meaning "to physically show" or "overtly display." Christianity must be a show-and-tell experience of Jesus Christ, the Truth. Albert Camus says it in more contemporary terms:

The world expects of Christians that they

13

will raise their voices so loudly and clearly and so formulate their protest that not even the simplest man can have the slightest doubt about what they are saying. Further, the world expects of Christians that they will eschew all fuzzy abstractions and plant themselves squarely in front of the bloody face of history. We stand in need of folk who have determined to speak directly and unmistakably and come what may, to stand by what they **have** said.

Paul admonished the church at Corinth to make Christ's life-style their own, or their church would die.

It is when Jesus Christ is seen as the Truth that the significance of the Ten Commandments becomes apparent. If the truth has to be lived in the sweat and blood of our lives, it must be lived with some guidelines.

The Ten Commandments? God, You've got to be kidding!

No, He wasn't. Some would deny the need for rules in the game of life, but Christ didn't. In His earthly ministry, He repeatedly endorsed the principles of the Ten Commandments as the pattern for living. In His Sermon on the Mount and in His repeated encounters with Jewish intelligentsia, He always upheld the words of the Law. More importantly, Christ stated, "Do not think that I came to abolish the Law or the Prophets; I came not to abolish, but to fulfill." It is in Christ that the intent of the Law was realized. In the Lord Jesus Christ those ancient no-no's, conceived on a granite peak in the desert, became the pattern for living.

This book is written so that the ancient Law will become contemporary truth. It is not my purpose to nail any spiritual hides to the ecclesiastical wall with ten legalistic nails, but to show the refreshing freedom of living the Truth—Jesus Christ.

In John 8:32 Christ said, "And you shall know the truth, and the truth shall make you free." Freedom is a subject all of us can identify with. The Fifth Dimension taught us that "People Gotta Be Free." At 5:30 we watch John Chancellor narrate the latest freedom riot somewhere in the world. During vacations we confront our parents in the attempt to convince them of our personal autonomy in matters of dating partners, dress, and hair length.

The popular cries of the college liberation front are freedom from cafeteria jello, from oppression by the administration, from super-snooper resident heads, and from the eternal ant. In some

subtle way we all desire the "Bronson life."
Remember that past TV series which
featured a mild-mannered Hell's Angel
called Jim Bronson? Bronson rode around
the country on a large Harley with a pack
on his back and adventure in his eye. In the
opening scene every week he pulled up to
a light beside a "straight" sitting in a gray
Dodge station wagon wearing a gray hat
and a gray suit accented by a Rotary lapel
pin. As Bronson pulled away in tantalizing
freedom, the "straight" sat drooling.

Does the Bronson ideal exist? Hordes of
young people have said yes and have
begun a new life-style based on the ethic
of "do your own thing." They take to the
highways in droves looking for a ride to
somewhere where they can work out the
implications of their new philosophy.

But the do-your-own-thing ethic soon
proves impossible and new rules replace
the old and mar the concept of total
freedom. Someone needs a new and
warmer bedroll, so in the morning he takes
the nearest one and is on his way. *First new
rule: Don't trust anyone.* A guy picks up an
easy make, but before he gets a chance to
score she knifes him and takes his money
to support a habit. *Rule #2: Only go to bed
with card-carrying prostitutes.* A young

man joins a commune, but is thrown out because he refuses to clean the john. *Rule #3: Stay with people who won't make you do the dirty work.* Regardless of the intensity of our search, freedom does not exist without boundaries.

If one is to be truly free, he has to be able to move without restriction within the limits of his freedom. The tragic fact is, sin will not allow that. After Christ pronounced freedom in Himself, some self-righteous Jews wanted to know what they had to be free from. "They answered Him, 'We are Abraham's offspring, and have never yet been enslaved to anyone; how is it that You say, "You shall become free"?' Jesus answered them, 'Truly, truly, I say to you, everyone who commits sin is the slave of sin.' " (John 8:33,34). Sin then, not the law of God, is what keeps a person from being truly free. As Paul explains in the third chapter of Galatians, the boundaries of the law are intended to display the exceeding sinfulness of sin and make the freedom of Christ meaningful.

The Ten Commandments are the basis of a moral law. Because man is free, he is also moral, and moral laws become essential. Moral laws preserve the natural state of man; they are intended to help him realize the ends for which he was created. Therefore, the Ten Commandments (or the Decalogue, as they also are called) are a prototype of what God originally planned for man. It was never God's intention for us to desire our roommate's success, lie about the number of pages we have read, or deface the sanctity of a future marriage in the back seat of a parked car. God speaks to us today with the same clarity and authority that those travel-worn Israelites heard when He said, "These words, which I am commanding you today, shall be on your heart" (Deuteronomy 6:6). Ultimate freedom in this life is to live within the boundaries of a moral code which God uses to insure our image as His intended creation.

Our acceptance of the limits that surround the truth presupposes obedience to those limits. This is probably the place where you want to put down this book. You've had enough of doing what you're told. The words, "You'll obey me while you are still living under this roof," punctuated the recent past. Throughout your life you have been beaten, cajoled, bribed, or embarrassed into obedience.

But obedience is the only way we can know God. Prior to Sinai He asked the Israelites for obedience. "Now then, if you will indeed obey My voice and keep My covenant, then you will be My own possession among all the peoples: for all the earth is Mine" (Exodus 19:5). God asked only for obedience, and the blessings of His covenant could be theirs. But of all creation we are unique, in that when He asks, we can say no. Our interest in number one is what causes us to say no. God saw the potential of that egocentric chaos produced by the Fall and prepared a guideline by which a man could protect himself from his neighbor. Civilization is based on this guideline.

We don't have to look too far back in the pages of history to find that Hitler proved God was right. When the limits of life, sexual morality, and personal dignity were violated, then the very bottom of a society dropped out and mankind crashed into depravity. He debased himself until the term *animal* seemed mild. It is hard to acknowledge it, but we all stand only one step from committing the atrocities of Nazi Germany if we disobey God's limits on our freedom.

God, however, does not want to have obedience motivated by fear, but by love. Psychologically, love is the stronger of the two emotions. Would you rather clean your dorm room for your chick or your resident head? Obeying is enjoyable only when it is done out of love. In the words of the Carpenters, "Love is surrender; you must surrender if you care."

This love doesn't begin with us; it started with God. He saw dirty, destitute, cursing Hebrews enslaved in Egypt and, in spite of their rudeness, gave them the precepts they needed to survive. Christ testifies to the love of God in John 14:21, "He who has My commandments, and keeps them, he it is who loves Me; and he who loves Me shall be loved by My Father." Our obedience to God's law must be total, because in the words of John Calvin, "God's law makes total claim on us."

Having established the validity of a moral code and agreed on obeying its principle, all we have to do is live it. That should be no problem because we are all professionals at living—we do it all the time. Yet time does not guarantee perfection in the art of living. Every moment presents a new challenge to the integrity of life. I suggest that integrity will never be maintained outside of God's law.

The apostle Paul said, "For to me, to live is Christ." In a simple formula he asserts his life-style was not his own but reflected someone else—Jesus Christ. We can know the truth, but the truth will never set us free unless it is lived. Living the truth is making a moral decision.

2
Love Story

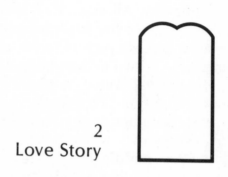

It was just a few years ago that America and the world went on an emotional binge. It was marked by crying and sobbing equaled only at the saddest funeral. Clothes hampers were filled with tear-soaked handkerchiefs marked with mascara and eye shadow. Theater tickets, obviously mangled and chewed by people in anguish, littered the streets beneath marquees that blinked *Love Story*.

Yes, the hackneyed Shakespearian theme of *Romeo and Juliet* had once again taken its toll of broken hearts as Americans turned out in droves to indulge themselves in an emotional orgy. The January 11, 1971 issue of *Time* magazine painted the picture more vivdly: "Wet-eyed men looking neither right or left. Girls carrying men's handkerchiefs, eye makeup gone, gazing at sidewalks. All victims of Erich Segal's *Love Story*, the five Kleenex weeper."

What makes a picture so popular that it grosses over two million dollars in its first three nights? What is there about a ninety-five-cent paperback book that makes it number one on the bestseller list for twenty-two weeks? What charisma does this middle-aged Yale professor, Segal, possess that people drive him into self-exile? The answer is found in that timeless theme of life—love. This fantastic emotion was best described by a young teen-age girl who said, "<u>Love is like swallowing a sunrise</u>."

Those of us who are in love can attest to the simplicity of the emotion. But at the same time, the world makes a good attempt to confuse its meaning. For example, you can buy bumper stickers that say, "Love it or leave it." Your stereos blare, "Let's get together and love one another right now." The FM radio station purrs, "Love is a many-splendored thing." The

New Left shouts, "Make love, not war." The theater page of the newspaper suggests *Love, Denmark Style*. And my wife constantly says, "I'd love to have some new clothes."

Even though the meaning may be distorted, love has invaded the campus of every college. Everyday I see it in a glance across a cafeteria table, clasped hands in the narrow halls, and a glow of happiness at a basketball game. Love is a permanent part of any curriculum, and it seems the syllabus never needs revision.

Is it any wonder, then, that God begins His moral code with an injunction to love, an emotion we know well? But does the first commandment say anything about love? Let's look at the statement of the Decalogue found in Deuteronomy 5:6, "I am the Lord your God, who brought you out of the land of Egypt, out of the house of slavery. You shall have no other gods before Me." Yet Christ, when asked about the first commandment, paraphrased Deuteronomy 6:5 by saying we must love Him with all our heart, soul, and mind. This is not a contradiction, because if the words of the first commandment are examined closely, they point to this conclusion. Christ makes it explicitly clear that living the truth begins with loving God.

Why should we love God?

Because He is *ours* in a very personal way. As you probably know, there's more than one Hebrew word for God. *Yahweh* is His personal name—so holy that some Jews would not even pronounce it out loud. *Elohim,* on the other hand, is a generic term for deity—any deity. It's like the difference between calling me "Cal" and "chaplain." I'll respond either way, but "Cal" is a lot more personal.

The awestruck Israelites at the base of Mount Sinai heard this voice say, "I am *Yahweh* your *Elohim* . . . ." God used His personal name to smash the barrier and speak directly as a Person to His people.

We can't truly love a thing or a blur out at the edge of the solar system somewhere, but we *can* love a Person. And Yahweh begins by inviting us to do just that.

After God has established His personhood, He sets His place in the universe. He says, "Never worship any god but Me." Now that is a very egocentric position for God to take. But he's not kidding. You see, if God is ever equaled by anyone or anything, He ceases to be God. The Israelites especially needed to hear that there was only one god to be worshiped, because they had been recently exposed to the multiplicity of Egyptian gods: Ra, Ptah, Osiris, Isis, and Horus, to name just a few. God was not asking to be just the chairman of the pantheon; He required obliteration of all other deities. He says, "I am who I am." Our love for God is not based on His ability to be number one out of ten possibilities: He is number one because there are no other possibilities.

Now if this line of argument has been too ethereal, not pragmatic enough, let me lay this one on you. We love God because He has proved His love for us as He did for Israel. He proved His love by being our Deliverer: "I am the Lord your God who brought you out of the land of Egypt, out of the house of slavery." God told those ragged refugees He had a right to a claim on their love because He had spared their lives.

But what about us? What has God delivered us from? The angel who appeared to Mary explained it all: "You shall call His name Jesus, for it is He who will save His people from their sins" (Matthew 1:21). Through Christ, God claims our love. We love not because it is a rule, but out of a response to a greater love.

If the sacrifice of Calvary cannot be seen as an act of love, it loses its meaning, and we are left with the antithesis of love—loneliness. Loneliness for the college student is probably best described by the cafeteria hamburgers on Saturday night. You open the bun, and there's nothing there.

Sadly enough, when carnal man cannot apprehend God's love, he retreats inward to find himself, but he is never seen again. Henry Kissinger said, "Our generation is the first to find that the road is endless, that in traveling it we will not find our utopia but ourselves. The realization of our essential loneliness accounts for so much of the frustration and rage of our time." The Beatles understood this loneliness years ago when they wrote "Eleanor Rigby."

Eleanor Rigby died in the church and was buried
Along with her name. Nobody came.
Father McKenzie wiping the dirt from his hands
As he walks from the grave. No one was saved.
All the lonely people: where do they all come from?

Life without God's love is a cheap imitation of the original.

Why should God deliver us or even want our love? The Word says it is His nature to love: "God is love." That means that all God is and does is done out of love. We have a God of character, because He can be angry, amused, hurt, jealous, and compassionate, all within the context of love. This is a difficult concept for us to grasp, because for us love is usually characterized by smashy lips and nibbly ears. You know, if He is a "loving God," then all He does is gush love all the time.

Or we go to the other extreme and anthropomorphize God until He becomes a recluse, a Howard Hughes who only makes long-distance calls to us when He's angry.

We must admit that what we speculate about God is ultimately unimportant. What *is,* is important. With this in mind, the statement "God is love" has to be more than a beginner's memory verse—it is the very basis of our faith.

Practically speaking, how can we love God on campus? We begin to love God by spending time with Him. When you exchange love with someone, you carve up your life-style so that every available minute is spent together. Some couples must be with each other at least eighteen hours a day. We go to the registrar's office each semester and schedule our lives for the next three months, but somehow we forget to program God into our lives. It takes time to get to know someone.

Once we spend time with God, it is the creativity of the Holy Spirit that will help us express our love for Him. We need this creativity, because we have such a limited number of human expressions for love. We give kisses, flowers, and boxes of candy, all of which become old hat after awhile. But loving God never degenerates into a hackneyed routine because we constantly meet people. The uniqueness of loving different personalities through Christ provides the zest of our love relationship with God.

We often make the mistake of thinking God is looking for *perfection* in our love. Actually He is looking for *totality*. Moses said to those sunbaked Israelites, "O Israel, listen: Jehovah is our God, Jehovah alone. You must love him with *all* your heart, soul, and might" (Deuteronomy 6:4,5 *Living Bible*). Loving God is loving with every fiber of your being. You can't love your future marriage partner with just your mind; you can't love him with just your hands; you can't love him with just your emotions. You must love him with every part of you, or the union will fail out of boredom and frustration. As a person, you have many parts; God doesn't want to be loved by just one. He wants to be loved as you would love anyone else. The crippled hymn writer, Isaac Watts, understood this when he wrote the final verse of "When I Survey the Wondrous Cross."

Were the whole realm of nature mine,
That were a present far too small;
Love so amazing, so divine,
Demands my soul, my life, my all.

The ramifications of this are immense when we consider what it means to live the truth. Specifically, it means you can never lie to your parents about that weekend—if you love God. You will find it difficult to walk out with a library magazine—if you love God. You cannot "use" that guy to get someone else—if you love God. The Ten Commandments lead off with a single commandment which, if kept, makes the remaining nine unneccessary.

Ali McGraw and Ryan O'Neal just didn't make it with their attempted portrait of love. As time has eroded their fame and fortune, time will bury our human love. But the greatest love story ever is a continuous showing.

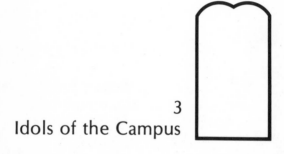

3
Idols of the Campus

Idols on a Christian campus? In the words of Brother Leroy, pastor of the Church of What's Happening Now, "Ridiculous!" Idols are for the occult or paganism—never Christianity.

And if we were to be perfectly honest, we would have to admit the second commandment doesn't really seem to apply to us! "You shall not make for yourself an idol, or any likeness of what is in heaven above or on the earth beneath or in the water under the earth. You shall not worship them or serve them; for I, the Lord your God, am a jealous God" (Deuterono-my 20:5). Right now you're sinking back in that orange air chair thinking God can't even hold you for questioning on this one.

But idolatry is not practiced only by bending a knee before a gold shrine or mumbling words to a wooden statue; idol-atry is ultimately a function of the mind. In idolatry the mind is giving assent to a symbol which represents the reality being worshiped.

If so, our society is indeed guilty of idol worship. Vance Packard capitalized on this in *The Status Seekers.* In it he exposes the gods of success and the way they are wor-shiped. For example, he cites the tech-niques used by builders to sell homes to people seeking social status:

A great deal of thought, on the part of builders, has gone into finding symbols of higher status that will provoke gasps of pleasure from prospective buyers. A Dallas builder, specializing in catering to businessmen who feel the need for homes in the $100,000-to-$250,000 bracket, has built one section that he calls "President's Row" because so many heads of companies live there. The houses he builds have such distinctive touches as his and her bathrooms, color television in the bedroom ceiling, push-button drapes, air-conditioned dog houses, authentic soda fountains, and hallway fountains. "Our clients," he says, "like these littler touches of plushiness."

So we sit and watch our society run pell-mell to offer itself up as a living sacrifice on the altar of the social register.

In this contemporary idolatry the symbol has become more important than the object it represents. No one would dispute the desirability of success, but if the symbol of that success is an unbearable $250-per-month payment on a Lincoln Continental, the symbol becomes paramount. Essentially, the second commandment says God is the object of our worship. When a symbol for that worship becomes more important than God Himself, we cease to live the truth and begin to die a lie. The apostle John said it perfectly, "Dear children, keep away from anything that might take God's place in your hearts" (Living Bible).

As I mentioned in the last chapter, the background of these fugitive Israelites made necessary the words of the second commandment. They recently had trudged out of an area beset with African deities characterized by bestial emblems and some new gods introduced by the Shepherd Dynasty. They had witnessed every conceivable method of pagan worship involving animal and human sacrifices. Now God prohibited these practices with language they understood: "You shall not make yourself an idol . . . You shall not worship them or serve them." These taboos were not selfish or a defense of monotheism, but were rather the result of holy jealousy.

It is hard for us to believe God is jealous. Jealousy, in our experience, is identified with the stamping feet and wild screams of a selfish child. But the Hebrew word *gana* meaning "jealous," also can be translated "zealous." With this meaning, the emotion becomes a possessive attitude born out of a zealous affection. It is similar to the jealousy you would feel if you had to share the affection of your girl with someone else.

Even though the warning was given in clear terms, Israel continued to substitute meaningless symbols for the true and living God. It only took twelve chapters for them to collect their wealth and fashion a golden calf. Scattered throughout the writings of the prophets are repeated admonitions to forsake the bulls, golden calves, and brass serpents that littered their worship. It was not until the end of the prophets that idolatry was checked in Israel.

With the advent of the apostolic church, the practice began again. By the eighth century, idolatry in the Eastern church had become so crass Emperor Leo III issued an edict in 725 to prohibit all images in the Byzantine Empire. In pre-Reformation Europe the situation was no better. For example, the Cathedral Church in Wittenberg, parish of Martin Luther, boasted such artifacts as a fragment from Noah's ark, soot from the furnace of Shadrach, Meshach, and Abed-nego, wood from the cradle of Christ, and hair from the beard of Saint Christopher. It was the devastating preaching of the Reformers that God is a spirit, and must be worshiped in spirit, that finally emptied the cathedrals of their icons.

We lament the destruction of such exquisite art, but we rejoice in the freedom of discovering divine truth.

After patting ourselves on the back for successfully waging this holy war on idols, we'd better look again. Pagan practices do exist, even within the boundaries of traditional Christianity. The Christianity I know best is found on an evangelical campus. Come with me for a tour of the idols of the campus.

Our first stop is at a residence hall. Here we find the idol of the dormitory erected. The dorm is a place where you carry in phone booths, stop signs, posters, and fire hydrants to make it more like the home you have always wanted. But the best part of the dorm is the people who live there. In spite of personality conflicts, one of the greatest attributes of your living quarters is the opportunity to make lasting friendships.

Aren't these friendships one of the reasons you gave God and your family for deciding to go to college? You saw in this varied student body people from all areas of the country and world and anticipated a wealth of information and even spiritual help. Those you live closest to become an intimate part of your life as you share birthday cakes, keys to your car, and occasionally a few dollars.

But these close friends become idols if they get attention before God does. For the sake of social acceptance, you follow the crowd almost wherever it goes. You don't have to work on the security force to know some of the crowds are going in the wrong direction. The empty liquor bottles, the smell of marijuana, and the missing wallets all scream that some in our community need our help. Yet the group usually protects its members in almost animal fashion without an effort to break the pack.

God doesn't ask for neglect of the art of being a friend; He asks for tenacity in the art of being your own man. There may be those who tug on your coat and say in convincing tones, "Try it, you'll like it." Be a person with the pride and spiritual independence to say, "I don't have to try it to know I won't like it."

The second idol is the idol of the placement office. This is the place we pass by for three years but expect to hand us a job contract during the fourth. That small office represents the culmination of thousands of hours of work and an equal amount of money.

But you all are getting a little more apprehensive every time you pass that place. Rightfully so. In twelve months job bids for male B.A.s dropped sixty-one percent, and a staggering seventy-eight percent for Ph.D.s. Of the 944 men graduated from the University of Wisconsin in a recent year, only 174 received jobs. Teaching fields are becoming crowded, industry is closing, and you sit in school with a minimal undergraduate degree and a debt that keeps you awake at night.

Suddenly God shows up your senior year and says, "Hey, I have a job for you." You reply, "Sorry, God, I'm waiting to hear first from the placement office." At one time your secular vocation was going to be the most fantastic witness for God—now He can't even get your attention. The vocation has become the object of worship.

The last idol appears on the south end of campus. It is the idol of the unlit parking lot. That's the place where you see couples—then you don't. You are probably thinking now is when prude LeMon does his thing. Well, prude LeMon was a student, too, so he speaks more as a peer with understanding than as a Puritan representative of the administration.

What concerns me most is not the moral implications of your intimate relations, but the farce you make of serving God through a love relationship. You know the prayer, "God, please send me someone to love. We can be such a great team for You." Yet national statistics tell us that this high ideal will be debased by twenty-two percent of the girls losing their virginity before graduation and forty-four percent of the men having premarital relations.

The majority of you take great pride in preserving yourselves for marriage. But the evening scenes in dorm lounges would indicate some of you aren't preserving much. With our background of strong sexual taboos, we resort to practices revealed in a study reported in the June 1970 issue of *Good Housekeeping.* "There have also been changes in sexual behavior of students who have not had premarital relations: Many more of them now accept heavy petting and anything short of the sex act as proper standards for themselves."

Some of you walk the scholastic halls with a tremendous sense of guilt, because you have been worshiping the symbols of love more than the object. True love finds meaningful and satisfying expression within a moral code. God wasn't trying to be the Scrooge of Saturday night. He gave us a standard so we could gain full excitement and pleasure in the expression of love. Romans 12:1 asks us to present our bodies to God a living sacrifice, not to one another as a sensual fetish.

Loving God through purity of worship is

part of living the Truth—Jesus Christ. The second commandment is a guard against diverting that worship to any other deity. The idols we have erected on campus can be toppled by a return to true worship.

4
Profanity in the Chapel

It is a warm October afternoon and excitement pierces the air as the two teams line up for their last series of downs. The game is tied. The huge crowd is hushed as it stands motionless, waiting for the ball to be snapped. The line judges are in position, watching with eagle eyes to detect infractions. (Of course, by this time, you have all guessed we are at another cardiac-arresting intramural flag football game.)

The count is made, the quarterback cocks his arm, the pass is caught in the end zone—but the play is called back for holding. The accused player rushes at the referee, screaming an ear-splitting series of profane words.

Once again immature and boorish profanity has come crashing through the papier-mache armor of the Christian student. The sanctified athlete calls from deep within himself the bile saved for such a moment. "Fake," "phony," "hypocrite," flash on the mental screens of those who hear. Someone has once again made a farce of God's name.

From our childhood we have heard the third commandment repeated, an endless cassette in our minds, "You shall not take the name of the Lord your God in vain, for the Lord will not leave him unpunished who takes His name in vain." As PKs (preachers' kids), the absence of profanity in our conversations became our distinction. We did not even dare use *heck* or *darn* because they might be the marijuana of further language abuse.

Now in our new maturity, we uphold profanity as a legitimate release for cramped emotions. It has become fashionable to use God's name and coarse language to strip ourselves of psychological hang-ups. I have been in a number of encounter groups, and the "Christian" gatherings always attempt to turn the air blue with their words. Our words are not a release, but a billboard we erect to let people know what's on the inside. When a Christian uses God's name in profanity, he only justifies the statement of Christ, "Whatever is in the heart overflows into speech" (Luke 6:45, Living Bible).

Even though profanity does occur in isolated cases in Christianity, it isn't really a major problem, so why even write on it? Well, basic to those locker room no-nos is the concept of what God's name means to us. It would be interesting to write the word *God* on a blackboard and then list under it all the descriptive terms it produces in your minds. We would immediately create a list of what Francis Schaeffer calls "God-words." You know, nebulous terms like *righteous, good, eternal,* and *caring.* Even though these words are sincere, they still seem to stay stuck on the magnetic board in that primary Sunday school class. We need a God whose name shatters the glass houses of our real lives.

A name is very important because it stands for something that really is. The name Calvin, even though I loathe it, stands for me, a sawed-off Italian who looks like Sonny without Cher. If someone is assigned a title, we expect him to act accordingly. Can you imagine a *redneck* with long hair, a *hippie* wearing Florsheim wing-tips, or a *New Yorker* driving a pick-up?

Names in the Bible often represented the character or background of a person. For example, the name *Isaac* in Hebrew means "laughter" because Abraham and Sarah laughed at God's promise of a child. *Jacob* means "heel," because at birth he was clinging to his brother's foot. And *Esau* is rendered "hairy," because of his furry appearance.

For the Israelites at the base of Mount Sinai, the name of God symbolized their very existence. They were hesitant to even name Him because He was so big and awesome. The term *Yahweh* was used but could not be spoken because of its immense meaning. When *Yahweh* was written by the scribe, he had to be in full Jewish dress, recently bathed, and must never dip his pen in the middle of the writing of the word. If a king should ask for his attention, he would refuse until finished with the name. God's name was more than a word—it symbolized His personal presence.

With this understanding, the words of Hebrews 6:16 become clear: "For men swear by one greater than themselves, and with them an oath given as confirmation is an end of every dispute." If you make an oath, then, and invoke the name of God, you have linked yourself with an obligation to the Creator of the universe. And where do we make oaths and promises by the name of God? It isn't on the football field, post office, or cafeteria line. No, we invoke God's name in the quiet whispers of the college chapel. When we make those affirmations of faith without a sincere intention of keeping them, we become guilty of profanity before God. After asking for centrality of worship in the first and second commandments, God now asks for the integrity to offer that worship.

Isn't Christian integrity what the world shouts at us as we come out of the church doors on Sunday morning? We are either cowards or intentionally ignorant if we cannot see the credibility gap between what the church says it is and what it performs. Northern Ireland is bathed daily in blood by Christians who sight down a gun barrel at someone's head in the name of the church. As teen-agers we watched on our TV screens the drama of upper-middle-class white Americans standing on marble steps blocking a black family from morning worship. In 1971 there were ten major Protestant denominations that took their offerings and invested more than $200 million in twenty-nine companies which were exclusively making weapons for the Vietnam war. Elton Trueblood was right when he said our Christianity suffers from a "vague religiosity." We have stamped God's name on our foreheads, but we mock it with our words and actions.

It is all too comfortable to sit and chastise "nominal Christians" for hypocrisy and profanity in the use of God's name. What about our own profanity? We profane the name of God by calling Him Father without any intention of living in His family. If God is the Father, then we become children living under His authority. When the Father speaks and we don't like what He says, our first reaction is to leave home. We pray, "Our Father, who art in heaven," hoping that is exactly where He will stay.

Our Father doesn't say no because it makes Him feel good—He says no because it is good for His children. God essentially said to Moses, "Now if you Israelites will obey Me and keep your part of our contract, you shall be My own little flock from among all the nations of the earth; for all the earth is Mine." Nothing but blessing was in store for these children if they would obey their Father. But they did not like what He said and decided to leave home, so they wandered for forty years still carrying the banner at the front of the column which said, "Here come the children of God."

Among us are children of God who are spiritual runaways because something God the Father said rubbed them the wrong way. They are usually in a Christian college because their parents or pastor thought it would be a fantastic nine-month youth camp. They walk out of the bookstore with "borrowed" pens and books, break into offices to steal tests, and write seventh-grade graffiti on the bathroom walls. But aren't these people all Christians?

Those of us who consider ourselves "straight" shake our heads and tsk-tsk at such actions, but haven't we been part of them? The family of God is concerned about all its members. Paul said in the book of Romans, "When God's children are in need, you be the one to help them out." If we call God Father, we had better be ready to minister to everyone in our family. The words from the hymn "We Beseech Thee, Hear Us" in the Broadway production of *Godspell* perfectly portrays this family relationship.

Father, hear Thy children's call;
Humbly at Thy feet we fall;
Prodigals, confessing all,
We beseech Thee, hear us.

We Thy call have disobeyed,
Into paths of sin have strayed,
And repentance have delayed.
We beseech Thee, hear us.

We also profane the name of God by calling Him *King*, yet refusing Him the lordship of our little kingdom. Some of us don't need a Lord for the campus kingdom or the one that exists within us, because we have filled that position with our ego. Let's face it, who wants a Lord when he's got it made—private car, twenty dollars a week from home, and dating a good-looking Southern belle. We have developed an inverse ratio between financial prosperity and spiritual necessity. God can never be King until we dethrone ourselves.

We do this spiritually, too. As we spend

time with our Christians friends we feel less need to work at Christianity. There is no reason why a Christian fellowship cannot exude the very essence of Christ if we become intent on living truth. I'm wondering how many of us will be in that group described by Christ in Matthew 7:21 (Living Bible): "Not all who sound religious are really godly people. They may refer to me as 'Lord,' but still won't get to heaven."

Then there are those who call Him Savior, yet take His name in vain because they have no plans to be saved from anything. *Saved* is a term that has been shouted at us, handed to us, and sung by us, yet it escapes the experience of many. We would be astounded if we could see each other as God sees us, wrapped in the filthy rags of our phoniness. I have counseled with persons on campus who reluctantly admit their rejection of Christ. But life goes on for them in its routine of classes and cafeteria without their being confronted with their profanity in calling God Savior.

Profanity does exist among Christians. It may not be found in the anger of a roommate's remark or even in the heated competition of intramural sports, but it does exist in the insincere use of God's name. May the Holy Spirit clean our mouths and preserve the integrity of our commitment to live the truth.

5

The Day Bedside Assembly Closed Its Doors

Two college students were talking at breakfast one Monday morning. The conversation suddenly switched from Saturday night with the chicks to Sunday morning with the Lord.

"Hey, where'd you go to church yesterday?"

"Oh, I went to Bedside Assembly where Rev. Spring is the pastor."

You now find yourself in that blissful state of do-what-you-want Sundays. No one bounds into your room at the break of day to wake you up. No one gives a minute-by-minute countdown until Sunday school so you'll be ready on time. No one sends you cards when you're absent or even cares if you make it into the pew. So you snuggle down even deeper into those warm blankets as your mind drifts into the oblivion produced by the Sunday morning quiet of the dorm.

You are probably reacting to a negative concept of Sunday. Many of us have had to observe an unwritten list of commandments for the observance of the Sabbath. "Thou shalt not watch sports on TV. Thou shalt not read the comic sections of the Sunday paper. Thou shalt not be seen by the neighbors washing the car." There are also positive edicts: "Thou shalt go to Sunday school, morning worship, choir practice, youth meeting, and evening service. Thou shalt do thine homework in the afternoon. Thou shalt take a nap sometime during the day if thou expecteth to get all these things accomplished."

This hypothetical list points up the folly of attempting to legislate what can and cannot be done on Sunday. I would prefer to allow the Word to speak with clarity on this fourth commandment: "Remember the sabbath day, to keep it holy. Six days you shall labor and do all your work, but the seventh day is a sabbath of the Lord your God; in it you shall not do any work, you or your son or your daughter, your male servant or your female servant or your cattle or your sojourner who stays with you. For in six days the Lord made the heavens and the earth, the sea and all that is in them, and rested on the seventh day; therefore the Lord blessed the sabbath day and made it holy" (Exodus 20:8-11).

Unreasonable? Old-fashioned? We must admit our attitude often reflects these words in *Christianity Today:* "Sabbath-day observance has become almost a joke in contemporary society." Once again, God is thought to be kidding. Some of us question His wisdom in placing number four in the same category with murder, stealing, and adultery. We see the commandment as narrowly religious, unconcerned with ethics. Maybe God is telling us something we are missing.

But look at the Israelites; they seemed to understand His intention. These desert nomads knew from creation accounts that it was God's plan to have a holy day once a week. Genesis 2:3 records, "God blessed the seventh day and sanctified it." God underlined His words by interrupting the manna supply every Saturday. Now at

Sinai, the Sabbath becomes a permanent part of the Law chiseled by the finger of God. God reaffirms this provision by repeating its necessity throughout the Old Testament.

Though God's written instructions were given to the Israelites, there seems to have been a universal awareness of God's scheme for periodic rest. The ancient Sumerians had a *tabu* day once every month to worship the goddess Sabitu; the Babylonians celebrated a feast day four times each month, and the early Hawaiians of the South Pacific acknowledged one rest period each seven days. All of these special days were marked by severe restrictions on work. These restrictions have been repeated throughout history with extreme interpretations such as Pope Gregory's in A.D. 600 which prohibited baths on Sunday—or the Puritan who hanged his cat on Monday for killing a mouse on Sunday!

In spite of the humor and absurdity of our observation of this day, God gives us definite truth in this concept of the Sabbath. Christ, questioned by his enemies, gives us some clue of what God meant: "Is it lawful on the Sabbath to do good or to do harm, to save a life or to kill?" Christ makes it explicitly clear that this day is not a pietistic limbo in which to indulge ourselves in "churchianity;" it is a day to minister both to ourselves and to those around us.

Specifically what does the Sabbath mean to us?

God began the commandment with the instruction, "Remember." He said, "*Remember* to observe the Sabbath as a holy day." The Israelites could not *remember* the Sabbath if they had never heard of it before. They knew from God's own example in creation that this was a major sign. God told Moses, "Tell the people of Israel to rest on My Sabbath day, for the Sabbath is a reminder of the covenant between Me and you forever." Therefore, between sundown on Friday and sundown on Saturday, these bedraggled travelers recounted their supernatural deliverance from the sun-baked slavery of Egypt. Every time they worshiped on the Sabbath, they remembered those great water walls of the Red Sea parting to make a highway of escape. In fact, it was this memorial practice of the Sabbath that preserved Israel's strength and faith during the Babylonian captivity of 586 B.C.

But Israel's practice of Sabbath-keeping has a direct link to us through Christ. It was on the first day of the week that Christ smashed the barrier of death and accomplished our salvation. Now the Sabbath becomes, in New Testament terms, "the Lord's day." Therefore, according to God's logic, each Lord's day we confirm the new covenant as we actively remember the resurrection. In the words of the ancient church father, Athanasius, "We keep no Sabbath; we keep the Lord's Day as a memorial to the beginning of a new creation."

How did you remember the resurrection last Lord's Day? Were you trying to remember between serves in that tennis game? Maybe you were reflecting as you changed the oil in your car? Sure, you can worship God anywhere, but He has already suggested a place—the church. The New Testament authorizes the church to take the place of the Jewish synagogue as we corporately express our remembrance of His sacrifice.

You must be thinking by now that I'm doing a commercial for your campus chaplain. Actually I am making an appeal, on the authority of the Word, for you to engage in divinely instituted worship. You

57

say it is impossible to remember Christ and His sacrifice during twenty-minute announcements or when the organist insists on making the sanctuary sound like a skating rink? Some of us can't seem to find a church that fits. Possibly we're four sizes too small, spiritually speaking. We may be looking for the right style instead of the right spiritual size.

Along with the requirement of remembering is that of resting. Here is where we all breathe a little easier, because most students seem to have little trouble with repose. I see you "reposing" during classes, in chapel, and always before Saturday brunch. Sleeping may come easy to us because it was, while we were home, one of the few acceptable Sunday activities. A Sunday afternoon walk through a dormitory hall reveals a lot of obedience to the fourth commandment.

But resting on the Sabbath involves more than sleeping. God's directive was that the work of the week be interrupted by a definite change of pace and activity. What God is insisting upon is the natural rhythm of life. Life cannot be a static line of the same events. It must be broken at regular intervals for us to maintain our spiritual and physical equilibrium.

Probably the most depressing three months of my life were spent the summer of my sophomore year when I worked as a lifeguard seven days a week. Every day my prayer list was headed with a plea for rain. After two months, I was completely exhausted from the monotony of my schedule. Some of us are exhausted from the monotony of quizzes, papers, and reading until we walk around in almost a comatose state. But Sunday doesn't help us because we date on Friday and Saturday nights, sleep and ride bikes on Saturday afternoon, and push all our books to that perpetual study hall of the week—Sunday afternoon. Christ said in Mark 2:27 that "the Sabbath was made for man, and not man for the Sabbath." We break the fourth commandment when we insist on making Sunday an extension of Friday.

There is far greater truth to this commandment than going to church or refreshing our minds—it is the concept of having time for God. Time, represented by that ticking device on your wrist, is something we constantly compete with but never beat. Students don't have time to study, and faculty don't have time to prepare what the students should study. To add to our poverty of time, we delight in activities which spawn committees—which only continue to waste time and mimeograph paper.

If God can only get our attention for a few moments every morning and maybe once on Sunday, then He is much less than the God of fire and smoke on Mount Sinai. Where are our priorities? It takes time to know God, yet he finds it difficult to work into the computer program of our college lives. What might the spiritual character of a campus be if each of us took one three-hour lab course called, "Prayer—knowing God"?

The first three commandments show God's character; the fourth gives the method for knowing Him. To you the Sabbath may be a remote term found in the frayed pages of a dusty Old Testament, but God intended the Sabbath to be an active method for you to know Him. Living the truth involves taking some of your precious time to know the truth. Maybe the words of the fourth commandment will echo through the quietness of your dorm room next Sunday morning and awaken you to the thrilling experience of being "in the Spirit on the Lord's day."

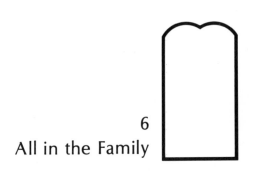

6
All in the Family

The library suddenly empties, the practice rooms become silent, and the cafeteria quickly loses its last customers. The college band refuses to rehearse and the science make-up labs are delayed a half-hour. Where has the erudite student body gone?

To face the boob-tube! They wait in gleeful anticipation to hear Archie say, "Edith, don't be a dingbat!" or "Look, meathead, you can talk around here as soon as you start paying rent." His remarks on ethnic groups produce either a burst of laughter or a blush of anger, depending on one's national origin. "All in the Family" is a historic TV success because it candidly speaks to us where we live.

Through the history of entertainment, one theme almost every audience identifies with is the agony and delight of family life. Our short television age has been marked with such favorites as "I Remember Mama" (at least the faculty will remember), "Ozzie and Harriet," "My Three Sons," and "Family Affair." So Archie Bunker becomes the latest national representative of a great American home as he and his long-haired son-in-law verbally fire at one another across the generation gap.

One thing you've got to say about Archie: he *is* the head of the house. When he says, "Get outa my chair," everyone moves, including the meathead. His authority is definite and precise. Whether he knows how to use his authority with any wisdom or sensitivity is another question, of course.

You are all a living contradiction of the idea that parents don't really count anymore. Their prejudices and life-style are indelibly imprinted on your personality. Psychology tells us rigid people are produced by severe or premature toilet training, and homosexuals probably had an overprotective mother. Your own attitudes toward political parties, golfing on Sunday, and going to X-rated movies are determined by parental teaching.

Even though we know parental teaching is essential to one's personality, the society of the seventies has demoted the rank of the parent. Unfortunately, some parents have brought this situation on themselves by forsaking discipline and taking up negotiation in the post-war mania for self-expression. As one distraught mother admitted, "My daughter's morals shock me, but I hold my tongue because she'd have a fit if I didn't." It is the vogue to use the home as a dormitory with the parents in the position of inept resident heads. Look around: parents are cursed, physically assaulted, and taken for everything they own.

Can you see why the world laughs at the words carved in stone, "Honor your father and mother, that your days may be prolonged in the land which the Lord your God gives you" (Deuteronomy 20:12)? Liza Minnelli chuckled at these words as she related how she had to physically hold up her mother, Judy Garland, after many

Hollywood bashes. Or how can this commandment seem valid to the disheveled dropout from society who stands motionless on the street corners of America reflecting on his income tax-cheating, beer-guzzling, spouse-swapping parents.

Naturally the world mocks the fifth commandment because its words strip nude the unethical character of contemporary parenthood. But it isn't our non-Christian society that invalidates this commandment—we do. It applies directly to us, because it is addressed to children in the covenant community. Paul was not writing to pagans when he said, "Children, obey your parents in the Lord, for this is right." Subjection to our parents is not dependent on their ability to be ethical, but on our acceptance of God's authority in them. The fifth commandment, then, is more than just a proof text for using a strap or for raising "good kids." It becomes a test of God's authority in our lives.

Israel especially needed to observe this commandment, or the very fabric of its small society would be ripped apart. They were nomads, traveling across an uncharted desert with a sense of supernatural guidance. But within their ranks were those who had grandiose visions of what things would look like with them leading the column. Anarchy loomed unless there was a chain of command. Someone had to have the final word. God supplied this needed authority by starting in the home. At the head of every family unit was a set of adults who were given divine authority. Exodus 21:17, Leviticus 20:9, and Proverbs 20:20 all repeat God's intention that parents have the last word in the family and that failure to abide by that word would result in death.

Not only the Bible, but the annals of history vindicate the concept of parental authority. The ancient Egyptian author, Ptahhotep, who wrote even before Abraham, said, "The duty of filial piety is strictly inculcated." Confucius, the Chinese moralist, based his entire set of mores on the parental office. The Greek historian, Plutarch, said, "Nature and the laws which guard natural order have put the first and chief honor upon parents." We only have to scan the World War II documents about German children turning in their parents to the Nazi SS to see the utter chaos that results when parents no longer lead.

Right now, we are painfully aware of the failures of the past generation. We deride our parents for the polluted air we breathe, their wars we are required to fight, and their moral code which we despise. William J. McGill, president of Columbia University, recently estimated that more than fifty percent of today's collegians belong to an alienated culture. In the words of Francis Schaeffer, "The modern youth movement finds in the universe no one home."

It would be foolhardy for me to deny these charges, because often they are true. But does their guilt remove the authority God gave them? God never promised us perfect parents. This present disobedience on the basis of the parental track record doesn't hold up with God. God wasn't playing Truth or Consequences with these Israelites at Sinai. Proverbs 20:20 says, "He who curses his father or his mother, his lamp will go out in time of darkness." We stand under the judgment of God when we usurp the place of our parents in the home.

But what about those of you who have parents who are not Christians? What is your responsibility before God to obey them? The Word makes it clear that parental authority is intact regardless of the parents' spiritual condition. Unregenerate parenthood is related to the Pauline in-junction to "be in subjection to the governing authorities" (Romans 13:1) as long as these powers are not contrary to the voice of God. Be careful in your judgment though, because God's authority resides within a parent not because he earned it, but because God gave it to him.

When we show respect and give obedience to our parents, we have done the same for God; the way we treat our earthly parents is a prototype of the way we treat our Heavenly Father. The apostle Paul makes it clear when he says, "But we should behave like God's very own children, adopted into the bosom of his family, and calling to him, Father, Father" (Roman 8:15, Living Bible). In God's eyes, it is inconsistent for you to repeat the Lord's Prayer in chapel and then use stinging disobedient words in the telephone booth when you call home. You can't tell your parents to "take a flying leap" and not expect God to take those words personally. Our relationship with our parents exposes the reality of our relationship with the Almighty.

So, you're having trouble with the folks at home? Let's face it, it will be a cold day in July before they can begin to appreciate your tapes of the Guess Who and your mid-calf, Army surplus trench coat. They will probably continue to complain about the length of your hair, skirts, and telephone calls. But regardless of your differences, you have a holy obligation before God to respect and obey their authority in the home.

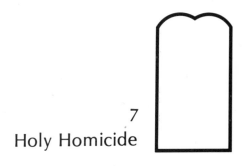

7
Holy Homicide

To preach against murder to students is about as profitable as preaching against male chauvinism to Germaine Greer. The last time anything was murdered on most campuses was probably when the cafeteria staff beat to death a new load of "mystery meat." It is a foregone conclusion that we would never entertain the possibility of taking another life.

Yet, even though murder may not have been our direct experience, we have acted it out many times. We were weaned on violent death in such TV favorites as

"Gunsmoke," "The Untouchables," and "Rat Patrol." After the tube was turned off, we role-played the parts in games of war, cowboys and Indians, and cops and robbers. Recently the media has been able to capture the very moment of death in such memorable scenes as Jack Ruby shooting Lee Harvey Oswald or the soldiers of Cambodia shoving bayonets through the chest of a Viet Cong. Murder has been graphically portrayed on the stages of our living rooms, and at some time we all have vicariously played a part.

We come to secluded suburban colleges and the wide, rolling lawns accented by shining glass and steel buildings do not insulate us from the terror of human depravity; the horror of Kent State really happened. No community is immune from what Reinhold Niebuhr, a theologian of the 1930s, called "the exceeding sinfulness of sin." From the moment God had to kick man out of the garden until man had brutally taken another life is just eight verses in Moses's record. Somehow murder seems to be the easiest solution to interpersonal problems. Our God-oriented, God-fearing, God-blessed nation has one murder every minute.

We are tragically mistaken if we think

the commandment not to murder is just for the illiterate, impassioned, or deranged of the world. God directed these words to a community bound by covenant to Him. They were not the scum of the earth; they were God's chosen people. Yet, God knew they had the potential for taking life with their hands and also with the intent of their hearts.

Your King James Version says, "Thou shalt not kill," but correctly translated it should read, "Thou shalt not murder." The Hebrew verb *shahath* means to kill without justification. Killing *per se* wasn't necessarily wrong, because God had commanded the Israelites many times to kill their enemies and even those who refused to keep divine law. Taking another life was justified only when protecting one's home or defending the name of Jehovah. When one killed without divine provocation, he had committed murder.

Which type of contemporary murder will I discuss: war, suicide, mercy killing, or abortion? I don't think we can begin to discuss any of these subjects until first we answer a larger question: How do we Spirit-filled Christians commit murder?

The apostle John gives the answer when he says, "Every one who hates his brother is a murderer." Suddenly all of us sit in a divine courtroom under investigation for holy homicide. It is holy murder in that we never pull a trigger or plunge a knife, but in a more fashionable Christianized manner, we destroy life with the violent hatred in our hearts.

Before the trial begins, we plead for a definition of our charge. What is hatred? John Calvin, the famous reformer, gave the best definition by saying, "Hatred is nothing but sustained anger." It should be clearly understood that nothing is wrong with the emotion of anger. God set the pace for us by having His anger recorded twenty-four times in the Old Testament. But if we let this legitimate emotion fester for a long time, it will create a boil which will eventually empty its gall on those around us. A homicide detective from Chicago described in *U.S. News* (February 16, 1970) the seething anger that produces murderous hatred. He says, "The composition of our cities is changing. We have a lot of people filled with frustrations and aggressiveness—all ingredients for murder: Two men argue over who got to a seat first in a restaurant—and one kills the other. The wife's slacks are too tight—so her husband shoots her."

Probably none of us has let anger grow until it consumed a life. We have felt like knocking a few heads together in the dorm or giving someone in the administration a small piece of our mind, but we've never been so angry that we would end a life.

But in God's vocabulary, murder and protracted anger are synonomous. It is hard to accept His definitions, because murder, for us, is aiming a gun or shooting an arrow. Yet, Christ verified God's logic in Matthew 5:21,22 when He said, "The ancients were told . . . 'Whoever commits murder shall be liable to court;' but I say to you that every one who is angry with his brother shall be guilty before the court." Once again, we are screaming at God, "You've got to be kidding." The logic of what Christ is saying is that the motive is ultimately as important as the act. If we refuse to accept this truth, we base our morality on the paper-thin foundation of situational ethics of guilt by degree.

Haven't we all proved what Christ said is true? Some of us can't walk down the halls without suddenly staring at the floor when a certain so-and-so comes toward us. What about the broken romances? You were always going to end "as friends" but have turned into bitter enemies. Then there are the caustic and malicious remarks passed in the cafeteria line or dormitory room intended to cut someone to pieces. Wasn't Christ right when He suggested we have murdered these people? They might as well be dead as have their dismembered characters lying about campus.

If this hatred is not checked, it grows beyond our ability to control it. This fact is sadly proven by some of the returning Vietnam war veterans. Harvard sociologist Charles Levy reported in *Time* magazine that the veteran is having a difficult time resetting his mind for nonaggressive civilian conduct. He gives an example: "Like many a Texas barroom brawl, the fight between a Vietnam veteran and a friend in the Panhandle town of Phillips was ostensibly over a girl. But by the time it ended, the friend lay dead of seven gunshot wounds. The veteran, a former Green Beret, dazed and thinking he had just killed an attacking Viet Cong, was stripping the body so that it could not be rigged with booby traps." Wasn't it an anger-crazed mob that asked for the execution of Christ above the rational choice of a murderer? Wasn't it hateful Saul who held the coats of those stoning an obviously innocent Stephen? The longer our hatred ferments, the stronger its deadly spirits become.

Am I now to let the harsh words of the sixth commandment become just another "hatchet job?" The commandment does expose the ugliness of our hatred, but there is a solution. The solution begins not with the injunction to "go pray about it," but rather "go do something about it." The apostle Paul suggests in I Corinthians 6 a face-to-face meeting with the one you hate as the first step. Colossians 3:13 says, "Be gentle and ready to forgive; never hold grudges. Remember, the Lord forgave you, so you must forgive others" (Living Bible). We sarcastically reply, "You're right, Paul." We cite the days, weeks, or years of prolonged anger that have built walls which seem humanly insurmountable. Paul is agreeing with you; humans cannot control their emotions in their own strength. We must swallow our pride and expose our trampled feelings to one another, not because we have the virtue of Saint Francis of Assisi, but because we possess the love of Christ.

We lie to God and each other when we secretly harbor feelings of hatred while congratulating ourselves for our fine expressions of Christian love. The apostle John said, "If someone says, 'I love God,' and hates his brother, he is a liar" (I John 4:20). The way we flaunt our phony Christianity must seem like a nauseating soap opera to God. Our hate invalidates that conspicious New Testament in our shirt pocket, our ministry last weekend, or our big offering for missions. God is looking for real people.

Now we can see the ethical demands of this commandment in living the truth. God is asking us to forsake our selfish desire for revenge and trade it for mature Christian love. Hate produced a Sirhan Sirhan who turned a celebration into a gory nightmare; hate produced sixteen million graves from World War II. What will *your* hate produce?

Sure, you've been hurt by someone's caustic words, but nurturing that anger will only produce "sanctified" murder in the eyes of God.

Is there someone you should talk with today? Is it time for you to make the first move toward reconciliation? Holy homicide is a serious charge.

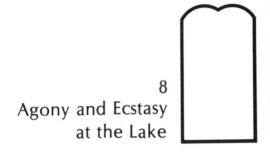

8
Agony and Ecstasy
at the Lake

This is the chapter we have all been waiting for. The seventh commandment has arrived, and once again we are ready to indulge ourselves in a youth camp treatment of sex. You remember the sermon titles: "Watch Out, You're Playing with Fire," "Back-Seat Christianity," and "How Far Will You Go?" You are poised for the standard admonitions: "Never kiss longer than three seconds," "Always double-date —preferably with the pastor's son," and "Keep your hands where they belong."

Let's try to raise this discussion above the

wrinkled-skirts/fogged-windows level. Instead, let's listen to what God says about sex and make some practical application. Let's give God a fresh chance to address us on this subject.

God begins by telling us He approves of sex. Possibly this thought blows our minds. Yet Genesis 2:24 says, "For this cause a man shall leave his father and his mother, and shall cleave to his wife; and they shall become one flesh." Even before Adam had a chance to kiss Eve hello, God had given His approval to the world's first honeymoon. John Milton beautifully captures this scene in his famous work, *Paradise Lost*.

So pass'd they naked on, nor shunned the
   sight
Of God or Angel; for they thought no ill:
So hand in hand they pass'd; the loveliest
   pair
That ever since in love's embraces met.

In spite of the Fall, God continued to record fantastic love stories in the Old Testament that make our literary efforts look like a poor issue of *True Romances*. We read about Rebecca running across a parched field to meet her love, Isaac, for the first time; the stirring story of Jacob, who worked fourteen years for his father-in-law to win his sweetheart Rachel; the tender tale of Hannah and her husband Elkanah who together encountered the challenge of a childless marriage. Sex in the Old Testament was both explicit and beautiful.

The New Testament speaks specifically of sex in relationship to the body. It was the New England Puritans, not God, who made "body" a dirty word. Paul said in 1 Corinthians 6 that God placed such importance on the body that it has been designated the home of the Holy Spirit. Furthermore, since the body is sacred, it is to be offered as a living sacrifice back to God. Paul calls this our "reasonable service." Some of our bodies are stretched out of their intended shape, covered with Clearasil and mascara, and seemingly embalmed in Pepsi-Cola, but they are still a divine reflection of God's original creation.

If God is so gung ho on sex and our bodies, why number seven? God wrote the seventh commandment, "You shall not commit adultery," in response to blatant abuse of sexuality. He recoiled against the sight of an Israelite leaving his home in the middle of the night and going to bed with his neighbor's wife. He became nauseous with the way women were selling their skin. He became angry with rebellious Hebrew teen-agers who marked their memories for life with torrid scenes of unbridled passion. The seventh commandment is a divine response to the selfish desire for self-gratification. Sex was to be expressed and enjoyed, but only within the proper form.

The form God approved for intimate sexual expression was marriage. Now there's a word that is becoming almost obsolete in our society. Jennifer Cavaleri and Oliver Barrett III changed marriage in *Love Story* to an "agreement" performed by the Harvard College chaplain. The United Church of Christ recently approved a statement that says, "Sex is moral if the partners are committed to the fulfilling of each other's personhood"—pointedly omitting marriage as a prerequisite. And the representative of sexist Middle America, Hugh Hefner, continues to sneer at marriage as the ball and chain to the contemporary playboy. Somehow the seventh commandment is rendered a sick joke in our society.

Unfortunately part of our society that ridicules God's original plan for sex is the church. In the December 13, 1971, issue of *Time*, the religion editor makes an important observation: "Some theologians are challenging the natural-law doctrine that lies behind the church's moral standards. According to natural law, an act is wrong if it is 'against nature,' but the new moralists are skeptical that the church can be certain about what 'nature' really is." You don't have to be a Hebrew exegete to understand that God's "nature" dictated that only two people of the opposite sex are to share each other in a love relationship until death divides them. If it is "natural" for us to have a multiplicity of relationships, someone must explain how the misery of divorce, illegitimate children, and venereal disease can be the outcome of God's original plan. They are gross perversions of the Creator's scheme. God will hold the church responsible for twisting His words until their meaning has been squeezed out for the sake of popularity.

God asks for sexual expression only in marriage because we are not psychologically capable of handling a number of intimate relationships. What God is actually asking for is respect for the individual. The sin involved in adultery is not in the biological act, but in its degrading effect on human character. Sex is the most tangible way we give our love to someone. That giving involves more than our bodies—we give our most precious private feelings, the very essence of our personalities. When a person has sex with someone other than his mate, he has trampled on the velvet feelings exposed by his first lover. Of more lasting importance, the adulterer has taken on the reputation of a prostitute who degrades love to mere sensual gratification. The apostle Paul said, "Do you not know that the one who joins himself with a harlot is one body with her?" (1 Corinthians 6:16).

Degrading the individual is what God intended the word *adultery* to mean. Adultery comes from the Hebrew *naaph,* "adulteration." The term was first used in idol worship when the Israelites were adulterating pure Yahweh worship with impure dieties. They had, in effect, defaced what was originally chaste and clean. In the true sense of adultery, then, one defaces or wipes his sensual feet on the pure face of love.

When we see the deeper meaning of adultery, fidelity in marriage does not seem unreasonable. God's expression in

Genesis, "They shall become one flesh," gives no option for one to get tired of his marriage and move on to someone else. Marriage was never planned to be limited liability. "Until death do us part" smacks of finality, and rightfully so. If the finality is not present, marriages could be ended for such mundane reasons as overcooked spaghetti, unfixed screen doors, and dented fenders. *Life* magazine once told the heartrending story of Mrs. Wanda Adams who got fed up with the routine of a twelve-year marriage and three children, so she picked up her coat one night and never returned. When marriage is viewed as only a thirty-day free home trial, it never has time to find mature expression. You have heard it over and over, but take it from one who's into it; you have to work at marriage. Marriages are made; they don't happen. Sure, there will be fluctuation of feelings throughout a marriage, but the elasticity necessary to fidelity will hold it together and give both parties a chance to realize the beauty of shared love.

Most of you are not married (even though you're looking), so what does the seventh commandment say to you? It speaks of respect for the feelings of others and a concern for fidelity in pledged love. The terms change; in your case *adultery* becomes *fornication* and *extramarital relations* are *premarital relations,* but the message is the same. You, and only you, are the arbiter of your sex life.

I would be less than honest to say that I have never confronted this issue. While I was in college, there was a special place equated with sex—Fellows Lake. This is the body of water north of the city where couples came from all over the area. Behind our smirks and sly laughs is the truth; Fellows Lake was where our parents couldn't watch us, the dean couldn't hear us, and the police couldn't find us.

The paradox of agony and ecstasy is in these moments of seclusion. There are seconds of gratification and thrill that ignite your mind. Then there are agonizing minutes on the way back when silence stalks a guilt-filled car. You grit your teeth when you enter the dorm and say, "Never again," only to helplessly repeat the same words next weekend.

But Christ is compassionate with your need. He was especially understanding with people who couldn't handle their sex drives. He forgave the woman at the well and the woman caught in adultery, but said not to sin any more. Are heavy petting and premarital relations worse than lying or murder? No! They can be forgiven if you are sincerely interested in letting Christ change you. You keep telling God you can't endure the temptation. Christ followed His admonition on adultery in the Sermon on the Mount with the suggestion that if you can't control your hands, cut them off. If you have trouble with suggestive pictures, don't go to see "The Sin of Her Skin" and expect to keep your mind on pie and coffee after the show. If you know you have trouble controlling yourself in the privacy of Fellows Lake or some secluded road, try parking on the mall under a light. God can't get your attention in the heat of passion during a date. He wants to speak to you in the coolness of rationality before the date.

Why should I say such things to Christian young people? Well, the world keeps pointing a finger our way. In 1970 three out of every four students lost their virginity. Berkeley sociologist Mildred Henry has found that such changes in attitude are particularly characteristic of students from "fundamentalistic Christian homes." A recent Gallup Poll shows a twenty-four percent increase last year in premarital relations for students in evangelical denominational colleges. Is the world laughing at us? Worse, is God weeping over us?

Your sex life is your private business. Nothing in this book is going to make any difference in your private life—if you don't want it to. But living the truth has to extend into your private life, or the truth is never really lived; it is just play-acted.

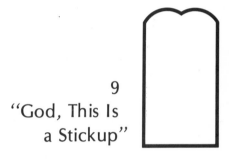

9
"God, This Is
a Stickup"

The eighth commandment, "You shall not steal," is probably the most widely accepted of the ten. Store owners at the shopping mall repeat this one as they pull down the wire mesh screen to protect their display windows after hours. The city police endorse it every night as they cruise the darkness of downtown alleys. Homeowners pray it will be remembered as they reluctantly lock the front door before a vacation.

One doesn't have to look far to see that the impotence of the eighth commandment has produced a padlocked society. We have made our homes and businesses into armed fortresses to repel the contemporary thief. People have even chained their ten-speed English biclycles to the refrigerator door, dismantled part of the TV so it looks unattractive to a burglar, and placed steel bars across the front door. A couple of years ago magazine reporters found that seventeen out of twenty-four apartments in an apartment house on respectable 78th Street in New York City had been burglarized at least once. They described one apartment which had been "hit" several times: "Apartment 2-B in that building is less a home than a jail cell, a nearly impregnable bastion defended by five locks, two peepholes, as well as alarms, chains, bars, bolts, and booby traps." We all shake our heads with insincere concern and say, "Well, that's New York for you." But the article goes on, "This fortress on 78th Street is not simply a response to a crime problem particular to Manhattan. On the contrary: nine other major U.S. cities have worse burglary problems than New York."

It would be an insult to the creativity of the carnal mind if we considered only burglary. There are professional thieves like muggers, shoplifters, pickpockets, fake advertisers, phony land developers, and quack doctors. Nonprofessional thieves make their appearance in even larger numbers about April 15 every year. The Internal Revenue Service tells us that if everyone honestly filled out his income tax form, within five years the national debt would be liquidated. It estimates that only seventy-five percent of total income is reported by those who list themselves as self-employed.

Isn't this discussion a bit too removed from us at school? We pride ourselves on keeping the thieves on the other side of the main entrance. There may never have been a Bonnie or Clyde or John Dillinger on our student roster, but we have bulb-snatchers raiding the main hall, wallet-pickers in the dorms, test-takers in some academic departments, and paper-plagiarizers in the library. The security force, locked doors, and chained gates all mutely remind us that the old nature is alive and well on most campuses. Somehow we dismiss this petty stealing as a community nuisance instead of community sin; yet, regardless of the size, shape, amount, or kind, an item taken from the possession of another is a gross violation of God's law. Detailed rationalization, unfortunately, does not erase these deeds from the memory of God.

We rationalize that the motive for stealing is really more important than the act. Right. When someone steals, he says that this possession rightfully belongs to him. He has become the arbiter of ownership. What the thief does not understand is that anything he has, whether stolen or purchased, really does not belong to him at all. As a matter of fact, before God none of us owns a thing.

The Word makes it perfectly clear that we stand in complete poverty before God. In the garden man was made the trustee, not the owner. Genesis 1:26 says, "Then God said, 'Let us make man in our image, according to our likeness; and let them rule over the fish of the sea and over the birds of the sky and over the cattle and over all the earth, and over every creeping thing that creeps on the earth.' " Jehovah used words like *multiply, replenish,* and *fill* to describe the relationship of man to the world. Man was never instructed to lay his greedy hands on creation and claim it as his own. The ownership implied by the eighth commandment is not man's, but God's.

Israel was reminded of Yahweh's possession just before they were given the Law at Sinai. God told Moses in Exodus 19:5, "Now then, if you will indeed obey My voice and keep My covenant, then you shall be My own possession among all the peoples, for all the earth is Mine." The psalmist boldly declares, "The earth belongs to God! Everything in the heavens and the earth is Yours, O Lord, and this is Your kingdom. We adore You as being in control of everything."

Doesn't the immature reasoning of the thief now become apparent? How dare he presume on the words of God to say as he steals, "This is mine"? The act of stealing is not vindicated by a mere desire for possession.

If we don't own anything, what can we claim? Did God intend us to acquire nothing for our own? Christ answers these questions in the parable of the loaned money. Each man was entrusted with a certain amount which he was to invest for his master. When the master returned from a trip, every man was evaluated on what he did with his money. With this parable Christ fashions the concept of stewardship. He tells us the results of this stewardship when He says, "For to everyone who has shall more be given, and he shall have abundance; but from the one who does not have, even what he does have shall be taken away." In the parables of the pounds, the sheep and the goats, the barren fig tree, and the unjust servant, Christ has taught that what we possess is really only on loan from God. We will be judged, as responsible followers of Christ, on what we do with these divine holdings.

What has God given you to care for? Some of you are looking at your frayed sleeves or putting your big toe through the hole in your shoe and concluding that God must not want to trust you with much. In spite of your present poverty, God has given you many divine possessions to develop as a good steward. The one we want the most, but have the least, is, of course, money. Acquiring money becomes a way of life. Students constantly look for work—raking leaves, cleaning houses, pumping gas. Some have an elaborate correspondence system going that always insures some replies wrapped in green. A more recent technique is to go weekly to the blood bank and collect five dollars for a donation of yourself. My wife and I were in the same financial plight when we were students. We were laughing the other day as we recalled the time we needed money for a Sunday night meal and crawled under the dorms to collect old pop bottles to hock at the local grocery store. We had no pride!

But does your penury nullify God's injunction to handle your money well and give Him ten percent of your income? When we neglect our financial obligation to God, we hand Him a note that says, "God, this is a stickup." We are robbing Jehovah in the same terms of Malachi 3:8, "Will a man rob God? Yet you are robbing Me! But you say, 'How have we robbed Thee?' In tithes and contributions." Sure, you still owe the business office for this semester, and five dollars to your roommate, but it is much worse to owe God. Have you robbed God of what belongs to Him?

Second, we rob God when we are poor stewards of His time. Time seems to come in such quantity that we fail to see the significance of using it carefully. It is fashionable to complain about lack of time, but what we are really complaining about is our mismanagement of time. The life span of the average American is sixty-three years. During that time we work fifteen years and five months, spend eight years in recreation and cultural pursuits, and still have five years to eat, three years to be sick, and two years to get dressed.

Has our time been used wisely? Have we used these fleeting minutes to glorify God through our lives? The apostle Paul said, "Therefore be careful how you walk, not as unwise men, but as wise, making the most of your time." Have you been robbing God of the time He has given you by repeated trips to the mirror to make sure the world whistles at you? Or maybe you have robbed Him with those hours before the TV feasting on the 1948 late movies and juvenile soap commercials? Christ set the example for us in John 9:4, "We must work the works of Him who sent Me, as long as it is day; night is coming, when no man can work." How will your timecard look to God?

Finally, we rob God by claiming our abilities as our own. Let's face it, some of us do some things well. Some are excellent public speakers, athletes, musicians, or actors. Your self-image may be a little down today, but deep inside you know you have always congratulated yourself on being an expert at something.

Unfortunately, our society seems only to

recognize those who excel in public. But there are people everywhere who know the expertise of quietly handling difficult situations, lovingly caring for children, and compassionately lending an ear to the lonely. Regardless of the visibility of your ability, God wants it. When you selfishly clutch it to yourself, you rob God of what rightfully belongs to Him. The apostle Peter said, "As each one has received a gift, employ it in serving one another, as good stewards of the manifold grace of God" (I Peter 4:10).

Yes, taking that light bulb from your suite-mate, removing the ash tray from Howard Johnson's, and swiping a pen from the bookstore are all violations of the eighth commandment; but the greatest thievery is perpetrated against God when we claim His tithe, time, and talents. Stealing from God or man always has invalidated any attempt to live the truth. The truth will be lived only in the integrity of God's law.

10
"Guess Who We're Having for Dinner"

A small group of students sit in the cafeteria eating dinner. Conversation banters from guessing what's in the jello to trying to describe the dean's sense of humor. An unusual hush comes over the group as someone passes the table on the way to the serving area. The conversation begins again: "Listen, have I got something to tell you about *him*."

This all-too-familiar scene has changed from *what* we are having for dinner to *whom* we are having for dinner. For the next few moments the character and reputation of another "friend" will be turned into the carrion of lies. Unnoticed, the ninth commandment, "You shalt not bear false witness against your neighbor," has been torn to shreds.

God once again takes all the fun out of the intrinsically enjoyable art of sharing dirt about each other. When God catches us in the act, we respond, "Well, God, everybody's doing it." The Russians lie to our State Department and the State Department lies to the Russians; ITT lies to Congress; Jimmy Hoffa lies to the court; and the petroleum companies lie to the consumer. We pay billions of dollars every year for the FBI to find lies and the court to punish them. Unfortunately, the popularity of lying does not erase God's injunction to tell the truth.

God's insistence on truth is born out of His ideal for humanity. For a person to be truly human, he has to be able to relate adequately to other people. When those relationships are severed by deception and lies, God's plan for humanity has been sabotaged. If we constantly need to check and double-check the integrity of our neighbor's words, life becomes frustration instead of freedom. Today we have border guards who check luggage, Internal

Revenue men who check bank accounts, and teachers who give quizzes to make sure you've read what you said you read. These are gross reminders that God's master plan for humanity has been destroyed. Emerson said, "Every violation of truth is not only a kind of suicide in the liar, but a stab at the health of society."

How is the health of your little society? Has your adherence to the ninth commandment made a difference between your life-style and your neighbor's? The apostle Paul said in Ephesians 4 that we have to be distinguishable from the world around us or we better take down the One Way sign. He says, "Yes, you must be a new and different person, holy and good. Clothe yourself with this new nature." One distinguishing characteristic of the new nature is the absence of lying.

This is what we have all been waiting for. Think of it! A distinguishing mark of the Christian college student that is not external. The general opinion seems to be that a Christian should not be set apart from society by length of hair or shortness of skirt. Unfortunately we often discuss only what a Christian is not and fail to give equal time to what a Christian is. I submit, on the authority of Romans 15, that a

Christian is known for his love—not the sickening sentimentality that surfaces at missionary conventions, but sincere love for a fellow Christian. God's Word definitely addresses Christian students and teachers on this point. God wants to know, "Have you given as much time and consideration to developing Christian ethics as you have Christian ideals?" The real danger is that both sides will run around checking shirts, skirts, and stereos while all the time trampling on those who are spiritually dying.

In a time of misunderstanding, whom have you had for dinner? Maybe you began the meal with an appetizer of sautéed administrators. For the main course, you gobbled up a fillet of resident head. Dessert was a chilled bowl of board members lightly salted with a few councilmen. If the statements you have made about these people or anyone else was knowingly false, you stand in the judgment of God.

The ninth commandment raises our lying from a behind-the-back stage to an actual courtroom situation. For the Israelite, God was making an important statement about his legal responsibility for perjury.

When one was charged in a Hebrew court, he had to be confronted by at least two witnesses. An instance in Deuteronomy 19 explains that if the witness was found guilty of perjury, he received the same punishment as the accused; if a witness made accusations for the death penalty, he had to serve as executioner. Throughout Exodus, Ruth, Proverbs, and Kings, perjury often was punished by death.

The ancient pagan world regarded perjury with the same gravity. In Athens it produced a heavy fine, and if it was repeated, the accused could lose all civil rights. A perjurer in Rome was thrown headfirst from the Tarpeian rock. Ancient Egypt inflicted a more visible punishment by amputating the nose and both ears.

But an Israelite was to think of more than the punishment when he lied about his neighbor. A lie was an affront to the majesty and veracity of Jehovah. In Leviticus 19:16, Moses told the people, "You shall not go about as a slanderer among your people . . . . I am the Lord." They knew the name of God represented ultimate truth and trust. Hebrews 6:18 assures us that it is impossible for God to lie. When we lie about someone, we drag the veracity of God's name through the slime of our sin. A rabbi has said, "Everything in the world God created, except the art of lying. That's man's invention."

How inventive have we been in the art of lying? Mark Twain sat down one day and decided there were 869 ways of lying. I'm sure I've used them all. We lie about each other by blatantly telling something we know to be untrue, sharing something that is true but will hurt, or by telling half the truth. We are adept at innuendo, side glances, and ending sentences with a titillating "Oh, I better not say that." We generate so much enjoyment in this pleasant form of sinning because we consider ourselves amateur moralists.

We fail to understand in the bliss of these moments that God wants to protect the character of our neighbor. Christ made this point in the parable of the barren fig tree: even after three fruitless years, the gardener continued to protect the possibility of growth. The gardener represents the ethic of love proclaimed by Christ in the Lord's Prayer, "Forgive us our trespasses as we forgive those who trespass against us." Paul said that when we slash the reputation of somone else, we have done the same to ourselves. Think of the worth of your reputation before smearing

lies on the character of your neighbor.
Shakespeare said in the play *Othello:*

> But he that filches from me my good name
> Robs me of that which not enriches him
> And makes me poor indeed.

We take great pride in singing the chorus, "I am the Way, the Truth, and the Life." Yet, when we begin to devour each other, Christ suddenly becomes not a way, but a dead end; not truth, but a lie; not life, but lifeless. His power to speak to the world has been invalidated, not by their rejection of Him, but by their rejection of our sin. Through our words of deceit, Christ becomes a laughingstock. Paul said in Romans 1:25 that sinful men "exchanged the truth of God for a lie." The apostle John backs up Paul in saying, "If some one says, 'I love God,' and hates his brother, he is a liar" (I John 4:20).

Are you having someone instead of something for dinner today? Must cannibalism be part of your life-style? If you claim to live the Truth, Jesus Christ, then you must also tell the truth.

11
The Perfect Ending

Happy endings are as much a part of American life as high-school football games or McDonald's hamburgers. Can you imagine a series on TV ending in tragedy? Have you ever visualized Big Bird of Sesame Street taking a fatal fall at the end of a program? Or how about Marcus Welby getting hit by a car in the hospital parking lot? Those old John Wayne pictures concluding with either a rousing charge or a passionate kiss typify our understanding of a good American ending. Our minds have been programmed since childhood to believe that Americans always win wars, successfully solve problems, and safely return from outer space. Unhappy endings are marked by groans and a toss of the *TV Guide* at the screen.

God also likes happy endings. After a long dusty trip filled with detours, Israel finally crossed into the promised land. Or look at poor Job, who came out of a putrid situation smelling like a rose. Or look at the New Testament record of people who had spent all their energy and savings on medicine without results, but were given new bodies by Christ. It is God's nature to write happy endings.

Through the words of Saint Paul, Scripture tells the perfect ending for any human situation. In his letter to the church at Rome, Paul is lamenting his inability to completely destroy his old nature. He paints a rather hopeless picture when he says, "So you see how it is: my new life tells me to do right, but the old nature that is still inside me loves to sin. Oh, what a terrible predicament I'm in!" But contrasted with his predicament is the perfect solution, "Who will set me free from the body of this death? Thanks be to God through Jesus Christ our Lord" (7:23-25, *Living Bible).* Can't you see the lights flash and the bells ring in the mind of Paul as he reveals the perfect ending?

This same perfect ending is found in the tenth commandment: "You shall not covet your neighbor's house; you shall not covet your neighbor's wife or his male servant or his female servant or his ox or his donkey or anything that belongs to your neighbor." This commandment appears to be another celestial no. But in these words is the perfect ending to God's moral law.

It is a perfect ending because if one conquers greed, he has reinforced God's teaching that the internal change must precede the external. All the other commandments (except the first) require an outward, visible change of behavior. But how do you know if someone is coveting? Coveting, having an inordinate desire, is accomplished in the privacy of our minds. I could be standing here right now coveting someone's clothes, and no one would know.

Christ always set the priority—change first within the individual. He said in Matthew 15:19, "For out of the heart come evil thoughts, murders, adulteries, fornications, thefts, false witness, slanders." The Word convicts us not on the basis of our act, but on the intent of our hearts and minds. The author of Proverbs has wisely said that "as a man thinks within himself, so he is" (23:7).

It is not enough to keep our exterior actions Christianized—to keep our hands off a roommate's wallet, ride the bus to church every week, never cheat on an exam. These are really only matters of discipline. An unregenerate college student could do the same. We may have Christianized students who are really spiritually rotting from impure motives and thoughts. Christian virtue is not so much avoiding evil in public as privately loving good. Christ repeatedly made this point in the Sermon on the Mount. The self-righteous Jews wanted to pin Christ to the Law, but Christ blew their minds by fulfilling the Law and publicly exposing the unrighteous scum in their hearts.

The tenth commandment makes a perfect ending, because when covetousness is smothered, it changes our self-concept, our ego. Coveting is extremely egocentric.

You may remember grabbing a toy from a playmate when you were a child. It made you feel good—it gratified your self-image. In high school your behavior didn't change much; you grabbed the best-looking girl to add to your popularity. Today you are in college and still want what others have, because it guarantees a good self-image. How many of you honestly wanted that expensive tape stereo outfit, electric air-blowing, vibrating comb, or the jeans with Clorox stains? We stand looking at store windows and drool. Why? Because we want to look good for our public. There is an ego to be maintained.

History has recorded this fact for centuries. How many wars were started out of greed? How much land has been acquired out of envy? How many lovers have been murdered in jealous rage? America's concept of manifest destiny in the mid-1840s, the bloodshed in Northern Ireland, and Joey Gallo's gangland murder in New York all proclaim that we are really interested only in ourselves.

From the day Adam and Eve thought they could become "like God," our old nature continues to dictate selfish protection. Victor Frankl, in his famous book *Man's Search for Meaning,* tells how this instinct actually maintained the death camps of World War II. The drive for personal safety was so strong Jews volunteered to shove and herd their brothers into the gas chambers if their own lives would be spared—perhaps only for a day. Before long the entire operation was maintained not by the Nazis, but by the Jews themselves. Richard Hooker, writing in the sixteenth century, said, "The greatest part of mankind prefer their own private good before all things."

It is evident this gross self-centeredness is not part of God's original plan: it leaves no room for Christ. The best cure for the selfishness condemned by the tenth commandment is the selflessness of Christ. James says we become selfless by submitting ourselves to God (4:7) instead of following our own desires. And the apostle Paul says, "Don't be selfish; don't live to make a good impression on others." He follows that admonition with, "Your attitude should be the kind that was shown us by Jesus Christ" (Philippians 2:3,5). As Christ becomes greater in our lives, we somehow become smaller.

If Christ has invaded our ego, it has been accomplished only because we love Him. This is the true perfection in the tenth commandment. What was begun in love in the first command ends with the same love in the last. God began these marble tablets by stroking love on the first line. The last line is a positive command to forsake sin not because we have to, but because we want to out of love.

Unfortunately, the word *love* has been used so often in our society lately that it possibly has become meaningless to you. God's love is anything but meaningless when we find our hate for a suite-mate being replaced by Him with loving toleration. God's love is not meaningless when we share Christ in a crowded bowling alley and watch the boredom of sin change to the excitement of salvation. Paul must have been right when he said in 2 Corinthians 5:14, "The love of Christ controls us." Christian love can never be nebulous when we work from the perspective of living the truth because we love the truth.

God didn't give us the Ten Commandments to see if we had enough discipline to obey. To stop coveting our neighbor's house, wife, or car because we have been ordered to is really only a military exercise. To live by the book is of no intrinsic worth. God intended us to live out these commandments from the impetus of a love for Christ.

The tenth commandment sends us back for another look at the dialogue between Christ and the scribe who asked, "What commandment is the foremost of all?" Jesus replied, "The foremost is, 'Hear, O Israel. The Lord our God is one Lord; and you shall love the Lord your God with all your heart, and with all your soul, and with all your strength' " (Mark 12:28-30).

The Christian life should not be characterized by constantly shouting, "God, you've got to be kidding" when we confront the demands of ethical living. We all stand on trial today. May the vast implications of the Truth, Jesus Christ, be lived on your campus and in your life.